W9-AWX-940

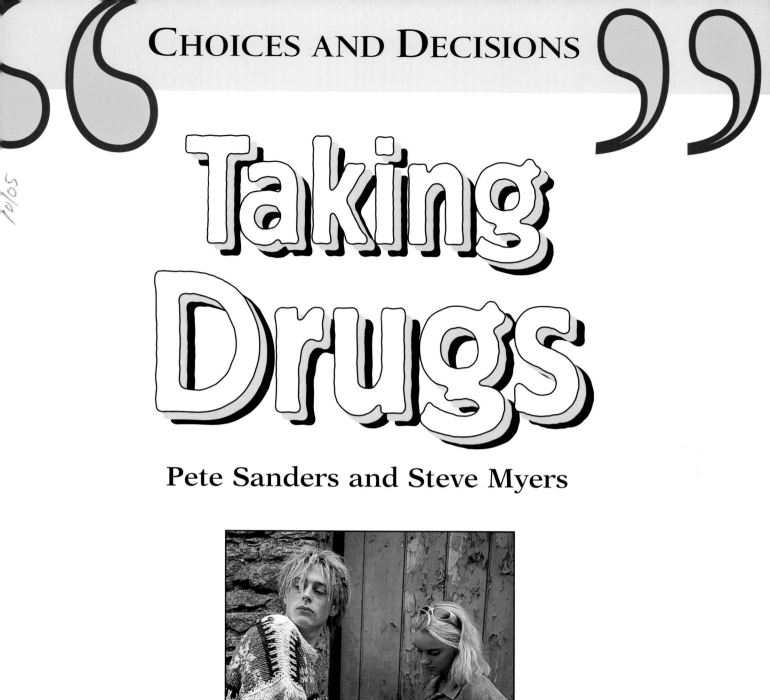

Taking Drugs

Pete Sanders and Steve Myers

Stargazer Books

© Aladdin Books Ltd 2006

Designed and produced by
Aladdin Books Ltd

First published in the
United States in 2006 by
Stargazer Books
c/o The Creative Company
123 South Broad Street
P.O. Box 227
Mankato, Minnesota 56002

Printed in Malaysia

Editor: Harriet Brown

Designers:
Flick, Book Design & Graphics
Simon Morse

Illustrator: Mike Lacey

Picture Research:
Brian Hunter Smart

Library of Congress Cataloging-
in-Publication Data

Sanders, Pete.
    Taking drugs / by Pete Sanders
and Steve Myers.
        p. cm. -- (Choices and decisions)
    Includes index.
    ISBN 1-59604-077-7
        1. Drug abuse--Juvenile literature.
        2. Drugs--Juvenile literature.
    I. Myers, Steve. II. Title. III. Series.

HV5809.5.S255 2005
362.29--dc22
                            2004061472

CONTENTS

How to use this book

The books in this series deal with issues that affect the lives of many young people.

- Each book can be read by a young person alone, or together with an adult.

- Issues raised in the storyline are further discussed in accompanying text.

- A list of practical ideas is given in the "What can we do?" section at the end of the book.

- Organizations and helplines are listed for additional information and support.

INTRODUCTION

> During our lifetime, all of us will come into contact with some form of drug, whether it be a prescription drug from a doctor, or an illegal drug.

Drugs can be extremely useful. Some are vital in helping people who are ill. However, abuse of certain drugs has become a major problem for both individuals and society.

This book will help you to understand more about drugs and the dangers of drug abuse. Each chapter introduces a different aspect of the subject, illustrated by a continuing storyline. The characters in the story have to deal with situations that you might have to face yourself at some point in your life. After each episode, we stop and look at the issues raised, and widen out the discussion.

By the end, you will know more about the different kinds of drugs and why some people misuse drugs. You will also understand the effects that drugs can have on society and on a person's life, what can be done to help drug users and to stop the illegal use of drugs. You'll find useful addresses and websites at the end of the book that can provide you with further information on drugs and their associated problems.

WHAT ARE DRUGS?

> A drug is a substance which, when taken into a person's body, alters or interferes with the way in which the body functions.

This effect may be helpful. Doctors prescribe all kinds of drugs to treat different illnesses. However, if used incorrectly, drugs can be dangerous.

Drugs have been around for hundreds of years. Some are natural remedies. Others are produced from plants or are manufactured in laboratories. You are probably aware of many of them—perhaps you have drunk coffee, or taken a pill for a headache. The most widely-used drugs are tobacco and alcohol.

Not all drugs have the same use or effect. Some are used to treat illnesses, helping the body to repair itself, or helping to prevent disease. Others are taken because people believe that they will have a pleasurable effect. One drug may come in different forms and strengths. The effect of a particular drug may also differ from person to person. It can depend upon a person's size, age, and state of health. If someone is not used to a drug, the effect on them may be stronger than it is on someone who has used the drug more regularly. One person may drink a lot of alcohol without appearing drunk. Another may drink a small amount of alcohol and become very drunk.

Many people enjoy an alcoholic drink, a cigarette, or a cup of coffee. These are all forms of drugs.

4

There seem to be a lot of different pills. Why does she need so many?

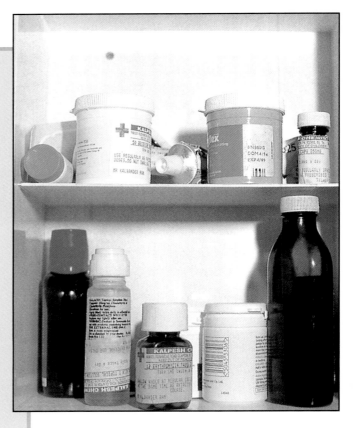

The doctors are giving Mrs. Young pills to help her get better.

A medicine is a drug or combination of drugs that has been designed to treat a particular illness. Some can be bought from pharmacists and other stores. Others are prescribed by doctors, and may contain very powerful drugs. You must never take a medicine that has been prescribed for somebody else, even if you think you have the same symptoms. Doing so can be very dangerous. If you take some medication and feel unwell, tell your parent or a doctor.

Taking more than the recommended dosage of medicine can be harmful.

Some drugs, such as cigarettes, coffee, and alcohol, do not state a dosage. This doesn't mean you can have as much as you want without any negative effect.

How long will Mom have to take those pills?

Lisa is worried that her mom may need the pills for a long time.

Some people need to take a particular medicine for the rest of their lives. When a doctor prescribes a medicine for a patient, he or she is taking into account several factors, including any side effects that a medicine may have. Some doctors have been criticized for prescribing too many drugs unnecessarily. Or they have been accused of repeating a prescription for a patient, without checking to make sure the person still needs the drug.

DIFFERENT KINDS OF DRUGS

> " There are hundreds of different drugs. They come in various forms. Sometimes they are powders or tablets. They might be liquids or even dried plants. "

Prescribed or legally obtainable medicines are produced to carefully controlled standards of quality. There are no such safeguards with drugs that are produced, bought, or used illegally.

The effect that a drug has on a person depends on the type of drug, its strength, and how much is taken. It can also be influenced by the method of taking the drug, the situation in which it is taken, the health of the person, and his or her motive for taking it.

Sometimes, people take more than one drug to achieve a particular effect. These drug "cocktails" can be very dangerous. Different combinations will affect people in different ways. At the end of this chapter you will find a list of the most commonly used and abused drugs, describing their effects and some of the problems associated with each drug. Remember that the effects of drugs will not be the same for everyone.

Drugs that are prescribed by doctors for medicinal purposes are produced and tested under strictly controlled conditions. Illegal drugs are under no such control.

The next day...

... David's friend Sam said he was going to a party at his friend Matt's house.

At Chris and Steph's school, Chris was upset because a friend of his, James Wilks, had been suspended.

Steph said that was nonsense. Chris seemed quite proud.

The school had been doing some work on drugs.

That evening...

... after school, David, Chloe, and Tom went to the party.

David told him that Sam had smuggled in some vodka, just for him and his friends.

Later, David noticed Sam and his friends Ahmed and Matt sneaking out of the room.

They found Sam and his friends in the yard, hiding behind some bushes.

Tom tried to persuade David, but he refused to listen.

All three were late returning from the party. David was feeling ill from the glue sniffing.

Suddenly, David ran upstairs saying he was going to be sick.

9

AMPHETAMINES Stimulate the body's nervous system and increase blood pressure • Taken by mouth • User may feel alert, confident • Continued usage can lead to irritability, inability to sleep, anxiety • Also known as whizz, speed, uppers • Illegal to sell or possess • Can be prescribed by doctors

AMYL NITRITE Used medically to treat heart conditions • Vapor is sniffed • Also known as poppers • Causes increase in temperature and heartbeat, giving a short-lived feeling of well-being • Can cause dizziness and headaches • Excessive use may lead to blackouts and vomiting • Currently legal

ALCOHOL Drunk as beer, wine, spirits, or alcopops • Relaxing effect • Lessens user's control over behavior • Too much makes people "drunk." • Side effects: nausea, headaches • Can cause liver damage • Can be addictive • Many deaths each year from alcohol abuse • Legal in many countries

BARBITURATES AND OTHER DEPRESSANTS Slow down certain body functions • Can have relaxing effect and may appear to reduce stress • Long-term use can lead to depression, forgetfulness, aggression, an inability to sleep without them, breathing difficulties • Overdose can kill, particularly if taken after alcohol • Tranquilizers are milder depressants, also called tranx • All depressants can be very addictive • Most can be possessed legally, if prescribed

ANABOLIC STEROIDS Powerful hormones • May be prescribed by doctors • Used by some sportspeople who believe they improve performance • Can have serious and irreversible side effects on user's reproductive system if not taken under medical supervision

CAFFEINE Drug contained in coffee and other drinks, including tea and some soft drinks such as cola • Mild addictive stimulant • Can cause increased heartbeat, heartburn, sleeplessness, stomach upsets

Different kinds of drugs

CANNABIS Smoked or eaten • Comes in solid or leaf form • Also known as marijuana, pot, hash, grass, and dope • Can cause a feeling of well-being • Large doses can cause vomiting • Can affect people's concentration and memory • Illegal in most countries

COCAINE White powder • Sniffed • Also known as coke or snow • May create a feeling of well-being and increased energy • Can damage the inside of the nose • Frequent use can cause nervousness, exhaustion, and hallucinations • Large doses can lead to death • Illegal

ECSTASY Tablet or capsule form • Known as E • Effects include greater awareness of surroundings, increased heart rate, a feeling of happiness • Popular on dance scene • Causes body to sweat more—can cause fatal heatstroke • Side effects include tiredness, depression • Illegal

HEROIN A brownish powder • Smoked or dissolved and injected • Known as smack or skag • Effects include feelings of warmth and pleasure • Addictive • Withdrawal causes vomiting, aches, sweating, and tiredness • Dangers from overdose and injecting the impurities that are usually mixed with heroin • May be prescribed by doctors • Illegal

LSD Pill form or as a piece of blotting paper containing the LSD • Causes hallucinations • Can cause depression, panic attacks • Some "trips" may be very unpleasant • Also known as acid, trips, tabs • Illegal

SOLVENT, GAS, AND GLUE Inhaling vapors of glue, varnishes, and lighter fuel can cause dizziness, hallucinations, and a short-lived feeling of well-being • May cause nausea, tiredness, headaches • Can cause death from lack of oxygen, inhaling vomit • Legal to possess these products • Illegal for stores to sell them if they suspect they will be sniffed

NICOTINE The drug in tobacco • Can be addictive • Tobacco is made into cigarettes and cigars • Smoking can cause cancer and heart disease • Legal to possess tobacco • Illegal to sell cigarettes to people below a certain age

WHY DO PEOPLE MISUSE DRUGS?

> There is no one simple explanation why people take drugs when they do not medically need to do so.

For many people, the reason is the promise of a "high." The high is brought about by the drug and changes the way a person feels or views the world.

Because drugs alter the way people feel, they can become a way of escaping temporarily from emotions or situations that are difficult to cope with. Other people may decide to take a drug because they are curious about the drug's effect and want to experience it for themselves.

Or it may just be that drugs are readily available. Wanting to fit in as part of a group can be a strong influence. If others are putting pressure on you to do something, it can be difficult to refuse. Sometimes, people use drugs as the result of a dare, as a form of rebellion, or simply because they believe it will be fun. Whatever people's reasons for starting to take drugs, they may not always be aware of the consequences of doing so. Abuse of drugs has the potential to seriously affect your life and health.

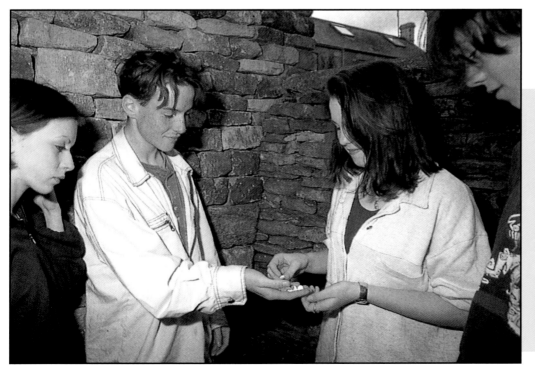

Some people take drugs because their "friends" do. They may be worried about what their "friends" will think if they refuse. It takes courage to say no.

... Steph saw Chris with James Wilks and his friends in town.

> Hi, Chris.

> So who's this, Chris? Your new girlfriend?

> No, just a friend. She lives near us that's all. Her name's Steph.

> So, Steph, do you want to have some fun?

> I don't think so. I know about your idea of fun, and it's not mine.

> I'm not scared. And I'm not a kid. What are you going to do?

> Come on, Steph. It'll be ok.

> She's scared. She's just a kid, anyway. Let's go, James.

The rest of them turned to leave.

Steph was unsure, but she liked Chris and decided to go along with him.

She didn't really want to, but everyone was watching her. She knew she shouldn't, but she took a drag on the joint.

They went to a disused building, in a part of town Steph didn't know very well. James produced a cigarette.

> But I don't smoke.

> It's no ordinary cigarette, Steph. It's a joint. Pot. Try it.

> Go on, Steph. Live a little dangerously.

> It's making me feel sick.

> Give it time. It takes a bit of getting used to. This is good stuff.

> I told you James was ok, didn't I? Come on, stay for a bit.

> It feels good, doesn't it Steph?

> My head feels really strange. It's late. I can only stay a little while.

Part of her wanted to go home. She didn't like the way the drug was making her feel. But she was worried about what Chris would think of her.

> I don't think so. I know about your idea of fun, and it's not mine.

The others are putting pressure on Steph.
Everyone forms their own opinions of what is right and wrong. If you are part of a large group, it can be hard to say what you think. If everyone is doing the opposite of what you believe is right, it can be tempting to go along with them. It is not always easy to stand up for yourself. It helps to think things through before making a decision. How would you deal with a situation where drugs are on offer and you felt under pressure to do the same as other people?

> Come on, Steph. It'll be ok. Live a little dangerously.

Like Chris, many people who take drugs think that they will be able to control their behavior.
But this is rarely the case. People who have tried drugs may think there are no long-term physical or emotional effects. Or they may believe that they are somehow different—that nothing can harm them. But the reality is that drugs can harm anyone who takes them.

New experiences are part of life

• Some drugs can make you feel good for a short while. But you need to consider the long-term and more serious effects of drug-taking.

• Putting yourself at risk by experimenting, as Steph and Chris are doing, is not sensible.

• It is important to understand the possible consequences of your decisions and actions.

DRUGS AND SOCIETY

> The way people think and feel about drug-taking varies a great deal. Some believe that the laws about taking certain drugs should be less severe. Others think that legislation is not strict enough.

Sometimes, illegal drug-taking is viewed as a problem that happens only in big cities or to certain groups of people. This is not so. People from all walks of life, of all ages and backgrounds, can become drug users. Drug abuse is a worldwide problem that affects many areas of society.

Supplying drugs has become very big business. The movement of drugs between countries—"trafficking"—is very risky. Drug traffickers set up very complicated systems in order to make enormous profits. This may often involve bribery of officials and the use of violence. Most countries have very strict laws with high penalties for those convicted.

Different types of drugs have different images. In many countries, alcohol is widely used in social situations. The fact that it is a very powerful drug is often overlooked. Nicotine is a very addictive drug, but it is also legal and easily available. Ecstasy has become popular with dancers at raves. Cocaine is often thought of as a "trendy" drug.

Many drugs are addictive and some, such as nicotine, are also readily available. Pop and movie stars are sometimes criticized for giving the impression that illegal drugs are acceptable. But nobody is immune to their dangers.

Three months later....

... Mrs. Young was out of the hospital, but it would be a while before she was fully better.

Something in the newspaper had caught Mrs. Young's attention.

Is something wrong, Chris? You've seemed on edge for days.

I've got things on my mind, that's all. Don't worry, everything's fine.

There's a story here about your favorite athlete. He's been banned for taking steroids.

What a cheat!

What do you know about it? They make such a fuss these days.

Steph was meeting Chris. She asked her dad if she could borrow some money.

That's the second time this week. What on earth are you spending it on?

Please, Dad? I'm in a hurry. Chris and I are going to a movie. It's my turn to pay, that's all.

Steph hated lying to her parents. For a minute she considered telling them everything.

You've been a bit distant lately. Are you in any trouble, Steph? You know you can always come to us, don't you?

Of course I do. No, it's nothing. Everything's fine.

Steph left quickly. She met Chris and Amy at the end of the street. They went to find James.

Ten minutes later...

... James handed over four Ecstasy pills.

We've got some money, James. What can you let us have?

Not here, idiot. Do you want to get me arrested? Meet me in the parking lot in ten minutes.

16

There's a story here about your favorite athlete. He's been banned for taking steroids.

Some sportspeople take drugs to enhance their performance. They believe that certain drugs make them stronger or enable them to run faster. This gives them an unfair advantage over their rivals. At most large competitions athletes are tested for different drugs. If their bodies are found to contain certain drugs, they may be banned from the sport or have their medals taken away.

Most countries have laws about drugs. These laws may differ from place to place. In the U.S., Australia, and the U.K., it is a crime to possess any illegal drug, even if you do not intend to sell it. Laws control the age at which you can buy legal drugs, such as cigarettes and alcohol. Alcohol is illegal in some Muslim countries. In Holland and some other countries, people are allowed to buy and sell certain drugs, such as cannabis.

We've got some money, James. What can you let us have?

People who make money from selling drugs illegally are called "dealers." Buying drugs from a dealer is very risky. There is no control over the content of the drug. Dealers may increase the price they charge as the buyer takes the drug more regularly. People often turn to crime to pay for their drugs. Sometimes, dealers become violent with people who cannot pay.

ADDICTION AND DEPENDENCY

> *Many people find it difficult to stop taking drugs, because they have come to depend on the effect of the drugs they are taking.*

Some drugs are physically addictive, causing changes in the body that produce a need for the drug. However, dependence on the feelings that some drugs create, or on the lifestyle and sense of freedom that some people believe they offer, can be just as powerful.

If the body has come to depend on the drug, it may crave more of it. Unpleasant sensations––withdrawal symptoms––are felt when the drug is not being taken or when its effects are wearing off. These can be very serious. With some drugs the body develops a tolerance, adapting itself so that a higher dose may be needed to produce the same effect. But this does not mean that the user's body becomes immune to the physical dangers of the drug.

It is unlikely that anybody who starts to take drugs expects to become addicted. For smokers, the addiction to the nicotine in the cigarettes may become the only reason they continue to smoke them. The only way to be sure of avoiding addiction is not to experiment with drugs.

People who use drugs to cope with difficult situations or to relieve unhappiness may become caught up in a pattern. For a short while, the drug will take away the painful emotions, but afterward people may feel even worse. They may also feel a sense of shame.

Two weeks later...

... Tom had arranged to meet David after school. When he didn't turn up, Tom went looking for him.

> I thought you'd be here. What's going on, David?

> I'm just enjoying myself. Here, try some.

> I don't want to. I'm really worried about you, David. Look at this place. These needles are really dangerous.

David had refused to listen. Later, at home, Tom overheard his parents talking.

> David refused to come down for dinner again. I don't know what's wrong with him lately. He just seems to spend all his time up in his room.

Apart from the discarded plastic bags, Tom had noticed some used syringes lying around.

> Mom and Dad are worried, and so am I. I'm scared, David. You've changed so much since you started hanging round with Sam.

> I know. I've tried talking to him. But he just tells me everything is fine. It's difficult to know what to do for the best.

> I know what I'm doing. You think you're so good, don't you. You're not in charge of me, you know. Go away. Leave me alone.

Tom went up to David's room. He told him about his parents' conversation.

Two weeks later...

... on her way home, Chloe ran into James Wilks.

> You're Chris Young's sister, aren't you? Tell him that if he doesn't come up with the money, there'll be trouble.

> I don't know what you're talking about. Why would Chris owe you money?

> Just give him the message. He'll understand. And tell him he can't keep avoiding me.

James walked away. Chloe hurried home. She felt confused and frightened.

> I know what I'm doing. You think you're so good, don't you. You're not in charge of me, you know.

David believes that he is in control.
One of the effects of taking certain drugs is that they make people unable to think clearly. Their ability to reason or to make sensible judgments may be affected. Drugs such as LSD, cannabis, and alcohol can alter people's sense of reality. They may feel powerful and no longer appear to sense pain. Under the influence, they may attempt dangerous activities.

> It's difficult to know what to do for the best.

David's parents have noticed that his behavior has changed.
The craving for drugs can take over a person's life, affecting both the drug user and those who are close to him or her. But it can take a long time for others to become aware that a person is dependent on drugs.

Some drug users inject the substance into their veins.
If drug users inject with needles that are dirty, they may be injecting germs into their body, along with the drug. Sharing needles can transfer tiny drops of one person's blood to the other person. If the blood is infected, the infection is also transferred. This is one way in which HIV, the virus that can lead to AIDS, is transmitted. Needle exchanges allow drug users to discard used needles safely and collect clean needles, unlike in the photo (left). This may reduce the risks from using dirty needles, but it doesn't prevent any of the other dangers associated with illegal drug-taking.

WHAT DRUG-TAKING CAN LEAD TO

> " As well as the devastating effect some drugs can have on the body, drug-taking can cause many social and emotional problems. "

Many drugs alter the way that people behave and can distort their thinking. This can result in drug users becoming a danger, both to themselves and to other people.

This is one reason why there are strict laws about not driving or operating machinery under the influence of drugs. Depending on the drug taken, the initial effects might include feelings of power or pleasure. However, there can be serious long-term physical and emotional effects of continued drug abuse. It can even lead to death.

Heavy drug users may seem to care more about their drug-taking than about the people who are close to them. This can lead to the break-up of relationships. Friends and relatives may suffer a great deal of stress and worry.

If someone is found guilty of possessing illegal drugs by the police, he or she will then have a criminal record for life.

Obtaining drugs illegally can be very expensive. Some drug addicts run up huge debts. They may turn to stealing, and sometimes prostitution, in order to get the money they need to buy their supply of drugs.

Later that day....

... when Chloe arrived home, she went straight to Chris's room and told him what had happened.

What's going on? Are you mixed up with drugs? They say James does drugs. Is that what you're doing?

I never meant things to go this far. I can't believe he threatened you.

Look, I've been taking some stuff—"E" mostly. Now I can't pay James the money I owe him. I even stole some from Dad's wallet.

You've got to tell Mom and Dad. They'll know what to do.

The next day at school...

... Steph went looking for Chris. She was supposed to go with him to a party but she had decided not to.

Steph had realized how much the drugs had taken over her life. She wanted to stop.

Oh go on, Steph. Forget about everything else. James has got some really good stuff.

Chris said he couldn't. He begged Chloe not to say anything until he'd had a chance to try and sort things out.

I don't want to do drugs any more. I wish I hadn't let myself get involved in the first place. It's making me feel really low sometimes and it's affecting my school work.

It's not worth it, Chris. And I don't trust James. I've seen some of his friends —they're using more than "E." Be careful if you go tonight, Chris.

I have to go. I owe James money, and I need to try to sort something out.

Chris, this isn't a game you know. I want the money in one week.

We're supposed to be friends. What's got into you?

I'm out of here.

At the party...

... Chris offered to pay off his debt a little at a time. James just laughed at him.

Why's she collapsed? Someone call an ambulance.

There was a shout from behind the two boys. Amy had collapsed.

I've seen some of his friends— they're using more than "E." Be careful if you go tonight, Chris.

Some people think that a person who experiment with a drug such as cannabis will eventually go on to try other drugs.
Others believe this is not the case. The truth is that it is likely to be different for different people. However, if you have taken one drug, it may be tempting to try another. This is why it is important to think about the possible consequences of taking drugs and to know about the risks involved.

Drug dealers

Dealers may take advantage of the drug user's craving and their need for the drug.

● Dealers know that many users will not only come to depend on the drug itself, but will also rely on their dealer to supply it.

● Dealers can be ruthless in the way that they tempt people into starting to take drugs, and then encourage them to continue their drug habit.

● The user can become involved in difficult and even dangerous situations.

Why's she collapsed? Someone call an ambulance.

Chris is worried about Amy.
Illegally-produced drugs are not screened for safety. The drug that you think you're buying may not be what you're actually given. The effect you anticipated may be very different from what happens. It is possible to overdose on drugs. This is when a person has taken too much of a particular drug. The effects of an overdose can be devastating. It can result in death.

KICKING THE HABIT

> "Nobody starts to take drugs intending to make it a habit. Nobody expects to become dependent on drugs. Coming off drugs can be a long and difficult process."

Realizing that you have a problem, and owning up to it, is not easy. Doing something about it can be even harder. But people can and do stop taking drugs.

People are often frightened of what this might mean. For a long time, they may continue to deny that there is a problem. Most people need a lot of help to be able to cope without the drug they have come to depend on. Life may suddenly seem very empty without it. Giving up a drug might involve giving up a whole way of life that the person has become used to.

There are various ways that drug users can get the help they need. Some people spend time in a hospital; others may join self-help groups or receive counseling. There are many support organizations that can offer advice to people wanting to come off drugs (see page 31). Sometimes, people may not be able to come off the drug completely at once—it may even be dangerous to try. Under medical supervision, drug therapy may be used to substitute a different drug or to give a lower dose

of the same one. In this way, the amount of the drug being taken can be reduced gradually and safely, without the drug-taker experiencing severe withdrawal symptoms.

Telling someone that you have a problem with drugs is a difficult but brave step to take. It can mean coming to terms with feelings that the drug-taking may have blotted out.

The next day...

... news of what had happened was all around the school.

What happened? Matt said Amy was in a hospital and Chris had been arrested.

He wasn't arrested, but he was questioned. Amy had taken what she thought was Ecstasy.

That's awful.

Tom had told Steph about David and the glue sniffing. She had talked to David the previous evening.

Meet me in the churchyard after school. Matt and Ahmed are coming.

You go if you want to. I think I'll pass.

After class, David stayed behind to talk to his teacher.

Something's happened and I don't know what to do. I want to tell Mom and Dad, but I know I'll get into trouble.

I had a feeling something was wrong, David. You've not been yourself lately. Your mind seems to be somewhere else.

David told his teacher everything.

It must have taken a lot of courage to come to me. I can't promise everything's going to be easy, but we'll sort things out somehow.

Mr. Young had spent the previous night at the police station with Chris. They had let Chris go after questioning.

Why didn't you come to us before, Chris? I thought you could talk to us about anything. We would have helped you.

I knew Tom was right, but I couldn't stop. I feel so mixed up. Can you help me?

It's not that simple, Dad. I thought I could control it.

So did Amy. What will the police do now?

I think the police are satisfied Chris wasn't dealing. They want him to name his supplier.

Chris had admitted to the police that he took drugs, but denied being the one who had given them to Amy.

I've decided to tell them. James didn't even stick around to see how Amy was.

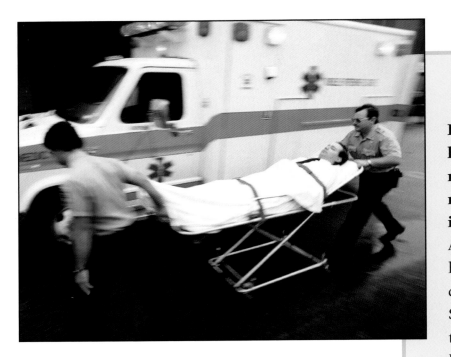

What happened? Matt said Amy was in a hospital and Chris had been arrested.

David is upset by what has happened to Amy. It has made him aware of the risks and the dangers involved in drug-taking.
A person's decision to seek help with a drug problem may depend on different factors. Sometimes, it can take a shock to make people understand how serious the situation has become.

You go if you want to. I think I'll pass.

David has now realized that it's up to him to change his behavior.
It can take a great deal of courage to stand up and face a problem, especially if you know that it will not be easy. But it is never too late to decide to give up drugs. Believing in yourself is often the first step. Seeking help when you need it is a wise thing to do.

A person who is taking drugs may already be experiencing feelings of guilt or shame.
Blaming someone for taking drugs will not help that person to get better, and may make the situation worse. Giving support to people who are recovering from drug addiction can mean being tough on them. They may appear to be in great distress. They could even beg to be given the drug or money to buy it. Saying no to them may not be easy—they may become angry. But later they will be grateful for your support.

WHAT CAN BE DONE ABOUT DRUG ABUSE?

❝ There are many different ways in which people are trying to stop drugs being abused. ❞

It may never be possible to stop the supply of illegal drugs completely. So, as well as trying to make them less available, measures are also being taken to reduce the demand for them.

Education is important in doing this. The more that people—particularly young people—know about the dangers of drugs, the less likely they might be to experiment with them. Education can also help to build self-esteem and enable you to be more assertive if you are faced with a situation in which you are being tempted to use drugs. There are many organizations that exist to help and support people with drug problems to come off the drug. Today, there is also more awareness about the

need to stop some forms of drug-taking from appearing glamorous. Some pop and film stars are involved in campaigns that help people to understand more about the dangers involved in drug-taking. In many countries, cigarette and alcohol advertising has been restricted.

Education is vital in the fight against illegal drug use. Many countries have special police forces whose job it is to catch those trafficking and supplying drugs. Despite these measures, illegal drug-taking continues to be a huge problem.

Drugs can have a devastating effect on people's lives––and not just the drug-taker's. If you're tempted to take drugs when you do not medically need to do so, remember that the effect you might get won't last, and it may not be pleasant. The long-term physical and emotional effects can be extremely serious.

Stand up for your rights

Learning how to stand up for your rights is a good way to protect yourself.

- Some schools invite former drug users to talk to pupils about their experiences. It's a good idea to learn more about the problems associated with drug-taking.

- At school or at home, practice how you could refuse drugs if they were ever offered to you.

- Remember that you always have the right to say no to drugs.

Mom and Dad were great, and I've been going to a counseling service the school helped to fix up.

Whatever the problem you're faced with, it helps to talk about it.
It is important to choose somebody that you trust, and who you feel comfortable talking to. If you think that somebody is dealing in drugs, or has a drug problem, it may be best to tell someone. This might not be easy, especially if the person is a friend. Speaking out could help to save someone's life.

WHAT CAN WE DO?

> Having read this book, you will now understand more about the different kinds of drugs, and the effects they can have on people.

All drugs can cause problems. Tobacco smoking has been linked to many major diseases, and alcohol abuse can do serious damage to people's lives.

Growing up is a time of many changes. You may be eager to try new things. People might suggest that taking drugs will make you seem more grown-up. You know that this is not the case.

It is important to recognize when situations may arise in which drugs could be around. You might want to think about how you would say no if you were offered illegal drugs. If you have taken drugs already, you need to think carefully about your reasons for doing so, and what the eventual effect might be on you and those you care about. Remember that it is never too late or too early to seek help if you have a problem.

Adults also need to be aware that young people will often copy what they are doing. If they see parents or relatives smoking or drinking, or even taking illegal drugs, they may come to think of this as acceptable behavior.

Young people and adults who have read this book together may find it helpful to share their ideas on the issues involved. The organizations listed below will be able to provide information and support, both to drug users and their families.

Canadian Centre on Substance Abuse (CCSA)
75 Albert Street
Suite 300
Ottawa, ON K1P 5E7
Canada
Tel: (613) 235-4048
Website: www.ccsa.ca

Cocaine Anonymous
3740 Overland Avenue
Suite C,
Los Angeles,
CA 90034, U.S.
Tel: (310) 559-5833
Website: www.ca.org

Marijuana Anonymous World Services
P.O. Box 2912
Van Nuys,
CA 91404, U.S.
Tel: 1-800-766-6779
Website: www.marijuana-anonymous.org

Narcotics Anonymous
P.O. Box 9999
Van Nuys,
CA 91409, U.S.
Tel: (818) 773-9999
Website: www.na.org

National Families in Action (NFIA)
2957 Clairmont Road NE
Suite 150, Atlanta,
GA 30329, U.S.
Tel: (404) 248-9676
Website:
www.nationalfamilies.org

National Institute on Drug Abuse (part of the National Institutes of Health)
6001 Executive Boulevard
Room 5213, Bethesda,
MD 20892-9561, U.S.
Website:
www.teens.drugabuse.gov

Partnership for a Drug Free America
405 Lexington Avenue
Suite 1601
New York, NY 10174, U.S.
Tel: (212) 922-1560
Website:
www.drugfreeamerica.org

Teen Challenge International
3728 W. Chestnut
Expressway, Springfield,
MO 65802, U.S.
Tel: (417) 862-6969
Website:
www.teenchallenge.com

Teen Drug Abuse
13223 Ventura Boulevard
Suite E, Studio City,
CA 91604, U.S.
Tel: (866) 784-8411
Website:
www.teen-drug-abuse.org

INDEX

Photocredits
Abbreviations: l-left, r-right, b-bottom, t-top, c-center, m-middle
All photos supplied by Roger Vlitos except for:
Front cover, 3bl, 6bl, 14tr – Image 100. 7br, 26tl, 27br – Corbis. 10tr – PBD. 14br, 15br, 20tr, 23b, 30b – Image State.
17tl – Corel.